# IMPEACHMENT

# IMPEACHMENT

## *Living On The Dark side*

Translated by

Carla R. Mancari

Celestial Literary Group

*Impeachment: Living On The Dark Side*



Revised June 2026.

# CONTENTS

# Acknowledgments

Sincere thanks to Mary Carpenter, who reviewed and edited. Her dedication is appreciated.

I am grateful for the revelation and gift of the Minute Meditation.

# Introduction

Impeachment and conviction of a President are a United States Constitutional means of removing an unfit individual from the office of the Presidency. Impeachment of a President is a sacred trust given to the House of Representatives and the Senate to convict. Impeachment is a solemn undertaking that this Nation must endure (when deemed necessary) if it wishes to preserve its Constitutional Republic.

*Impeachment: Living On the Dark Side* is a review of the why and how an individual would live in the shadow of the dark side. Why would a President of the United States ignore the rule of law? Why would an individual care more about self-interest than the oath the individual swore to uphold? *Impeachment: Living On The Dark Side* sets out to answer those questions. Covered also is the solution for an individual to re-enter and live on the light

side of life. Included are a review of
your Spiritual Center, the Minute Meditation, and its practice.

# 1

# Living On
# The Dark Side

Impeachment proceedings usually involve an individual living in the darkness with scales over their eyes, limiting inner vision. Darkness is pervasive in its nature and casts shadows. It is a cesspool of deceit, lies, and situations that individuals may weave to snare and entrap others. It is in the darkness that misdeeds are conceived and harm is inflicted.

An individual who chooses to live on the dark side is an individual whose consciousness' vibrating energy is continually being expressed in the darkness of negativity. Negativity is the destructive conditioned impressions used by an individual's conscious vibrating energy in thought, word, and deed. Therefore, everyone who lives in this world of opposites can choose to use their vibrating energy source as a negative or positive individual expression of consciousness.

The individual living on the dark side chooses negativity. The negative choice creates the individual's mental and physical environment. When the individual's choice is to express negative thoughts, words, and deeds, it attracts a restless, destructive nature (impurities) to the mind and body's vibrating energy.

What causes an individual to live on the dark side? By all appearances, the individual is often gifted. However, their gifts become tainted when used in the shadow of negativity. When the individual's vibrating energy is used negatively, the dark side eventually possesses its user and creates inner demons. Impeachment is the demons' nightmare.

# 2

# Demons

Demons are distortions of the truth. Demons are tormenting, distorted, harmful illusions of the individual's own consciousness' making. Living on the dark side, the individual creates demons through situations, persons, thoughts, deeds, memories, and expectations.

The individual gives demons life through attention, acknowledgment, and dialoging with them. The individual enables demons to assume their power. The power that the individual is giving away is used against themselves and others.

Demons thrive in darkness, isolation, and secret places. They intensify when left to their own devices and cut off from relationships. However, when demons of distortions are confronted with the light of truth, the distortions cannot be sustained.

If unaddressed and unaware, a demon distorts the truth. It gathers strength and creates a mind and will of its own. The more hidden and profound the distortions, the more dangerous they can be.

Demons prefer the darkness to torment the individual in the shadows of the mind. If unchecked, what hides in the shadows of the individual's mind can exert its power. When exposed to the light (impeachment), truth reveals and dispels a demon's hiding places.

Demons seek to destroy the individual's freedom and to frighten others. It creates the chains that bind and step into the tomb of possession through thoughts that are not real. Demons create a prison for the individual and those who the individual dominates. The first step in destroying demons is to cast the light of truth (impeachment inquiry). Whenever the light of truth (impeachment) enters the darkness, it stirs what hides in the shadows.

# 3

# Ego

The individual living on the dark side has a false sense of importance. It is a bloated feeling of false humility run amok. This individual is quickly taken in by the ego's many deceptive ways of engagement.

The individual may have rising thoughts of self-grandiosity. Ego continuously struggles with humility. Its goal is to eliminate any resemblance of humility.

The individual's ego continually perpetuates the individual's self-interest, always wanting to take credit for the works of others. The ego continually vies for attention, praises itself, and is always wholly centered on the "person" it believes itself to be. Ego sacrifices nothing, gives up nothing, shares nothing, and will take whatever it can get, whether or not it has a rightful claim.

The individual's ego always works for "what's in it for me, what can I get out of it, and how will it benefit me?" It is always me, me, me, I, I, I. Ego will eventually smother itself in its own praise and take down the "person" for which it pretends to care about. The ego opens the door for impeachment.

# 4

# Pride

Pride is an expression of the consciousness of a false sense of being independent. Living out of willful pride blinds the individual living on the dark side to the light of their prideful claims. The individual seeking worldly awards and recognition is a sign of immaturity.

A boastful pride works against the individual. A stiff-necked pride may slow down, hold back, or retard life's progress. The individual's opinionated pride attacks what it does not understand, narrows the individual's vision, and restricts the individual's ability to act rationally.

The arrogance of pride prevents the individual from clearly hearing what is said and closes the individual's mind. The stubbornness of pride may prevent the individual from seeking help when help is needed most. A prideful individual prevents mental flexibility. It invites the darkness into the crevices of the individual's mind and soul. The individual's arrogance of pride prevents the individual from being fully exposed to possible close relationships.

A prideful individual, steeped in their self-importance, attempts to hold to the illusionary things of this world. They believe their identity is confirmed by what they possess. With the attachment of pride, the individual may display and boast of material wealth while disregarding moral and spiritual worth. Self-pride collects that which goes from dust to ashes, destined to leave the individual in perpetual dissatisfaction. All the individual may accumulate; all the individual may accomplish in this world in the name of pride cannot ever bring the joy of living on the light side. Impeachment may be a wake-up call. It may be, but it is not guaranteed.

# 5

## Greed

For the individual living on the dark side, greed is desire coated with selfishness. Greed embodies willfulness, lack of trust, and lack of responsibility. It seeks to define individuals and the things of this world as "my, mine."

The individual living on the dark side is immersed in systemic greed that spreads its tentacles throughout the individual's existence. The individual's materialistic underpinnings rest on a large dosage of greed when the individual's fulfilling desires are a priority by any means, regardless of the effect it may have on the lives of others. If the individual on the dark side chooses to build a life with greed and a thought-focused mind, it is a life built on quicksand.

The mind left to its own devices, is easily distracted. The effect of greed is usually written on the individual's demeanor. The individual will often

24

show meanness and a lack of care for others' comfort.

The individual rarely smiles, and when usual respect is lacking, name-calling becomes a form of communication. Although the individual may believe they are intelligent and far superior to others, the individual's behavior is a sign that greed directs the individual's path and is overtaking the individual's life. This is a sure sign that even an intelligent individual may be incompetent when it comes to expressing that intelligence, thus, the need for name-calling. It is a form of intelligence warped by ignorance.

The individual may believe that greed is necessary to survive when, in reality, greed is what is surviving. To believe that it is necessary to indulge in greed to survive is a colossal joke being played on the individual — by the individual. The feelings of insecurities are endless, and they may easily lead to the creation of a bully. Being a bully is greed's most incredible creation and tool for getting what *it* wants.

# 6

# Emotions

Emotions are the rising of the many feelings that the individual living on the dark side may express. Anger, fear, and hate are a few of the emotions that may arise and be expressed. The intensity of these emotions may arise and be expressed according to the individual's state of mind.

The individual's expression of these emotions is usually wrapped in the complexities of the individual's conditioning and environment. The use and control of emotions may be learned behavior and is subject to modification. The individual living on the dark side usually lacks self-control over these emotions.

~~

## Anger

Anger is an emotion experienced as hostile feelings. Anger may be a negative or positive emotion. It is the intention of the emotional expression that matters. You may become angry at your child or friend, but do not mix it with hate. You let it go with for-giveness, dissipating the anger and freeing you from the emotion.

The individual living on the dark side cannot let go of the anger. The individual becomes a prisoner caged in anger toward self and others. Often, the individual will use the anger emotion to cause unnecessary harm in defense of the individual's own negative behavior.

## Fear

Fear is a paralyzing, restrictive emotional force. It can limit an individual's ability to act from a balanced state of consciousness. It can be so debilitating that it can override common sense, causing a stumbling block that would prevent an individual from moving on with their life.

Fear takes an individual on an emotional roller coaster ride through the house of horrors walled by distorted mirrors. Fear can hold the individual prisoner to anxiety that can arise when the truth attempts to break through years of conditioning. Fear can hinder an individual's creativity and paralyze the individual's ability to move forward. In addition, an individual becomes fearful the moment the individual must face giving up that for which an individual has spent most of a lifetime protecting: position and wealth. Impeachment may instill any or both of these emotions in the individuals living on the dark side.

## Hate

Hate is a sickness that infects the individual living on the dark side. To define hate as an intense dislike is putting it mildly. However, there is so much more ingrained in the hate sickness. It is so much more that it requires parsing it to be aware of its effect on the one who has the sickness.

Hate is a self-destructive emotion. It is a negative emotion toward self or others. Anger and fear usually accompany it. There is no stronger negative emotion than hate expressed in anger with fear. It can devastate the mind and body.

The individual who abuses the office of the Presidency plants the seeds of hate that raise its ugly head in the culture to the detriment of all those touched by the individual's sickness. The individual living on the dark side uses hate expressed with anger and fear as a controlling mechanism. However, hate has the teeth of an alligator, which may turn on the individual invested in hate.

# 7

# Imaginings

Imaginings are the illusions that occur when the individual living on the dark side is steeped in ego creations. Imaginings of self-importance may rise. Imaginings of being a great leader and doing great things in this world grab the individual's attention.

The individual's creativity may be heightened in the production of entire scenarios with great detail, playing out in the individual's imaginings. Imaginings may be very attractive and may hold sway for a time. The individual's curiosity to know the outcome of imaginings prolongs their multiplicity.

Because these imaginings are so thorough, they may be temporarily believable. Suddenly, the individual may believe their destiny and be convinced of its truth. The individual's Imaginings are temptation traps to step into. The individual may easily get snared by the imaginings of a mind living on the dark side that always is giving attention to self-aggrandizement. These Imaginings are the individual's alternate universe. Impeachment penetrates the individual's alternate universe.

# 8

# Rejecting Reality

Sometimes, the individual living on the dark side deliberately rejects reality. It is interesting because rejecting may occur when there is quiet in the individual's life when all is going well—there are no ups or downs. And yet, these are the times when the individual wants to return to the imaginings of the individual's own creation.

The individual's sanity may be questioned when the truth is of the individual's own making. The individual may struggle with the idea of being confronted with reality. The individual living on the dark side may play head games to convince others to reject reality. The individual lives a life of denial. Impeachment may be a reality check, but again no guarantee.

# 9

# Addiction -
# Emotional

The individual living on the dark side may be emotionally addicted to the constant feeding of a conditioned, pre-conceived, and deceptive emotional need. Addiction is not only a drug habit. Many possible emotional addictions may be every bit as strong as any drug habit.

Emotional addiction is as debilitating and enslaving for the individual living on the dark side as drug addiction. It takes hold of the individual's time and energy. One of the strongest emotional addictions is the need to feel important.

This need may come from the individual's early years of wanting to be noticed, lack of attention, or the feeling of never quite measuring up. Regardless of the ingrained conditioned cause, perpetually seeking ways to feed the addictive emotional need continues when left unchecked. Addiction itself becomes the priority. The individual's addiction to feeling important is subtle and often not noticed because of its deceptive nature. The individual may mistake the addiction for genuine reality. The individual wants to convince others that the individual is serving humanity when, in reality, the individual is serving their emotional addiction.

The individual's emotional need for importance has no reality in truth. It cannot be sustained and arises and falls into a mental state of chaos. It must be continuously fed anew. The individual cannot hold on to a feeling of importance because, in reality, it does not exist. Impeachment's reality is grounded in truth.

# 10

# Depression

When, for the individual living on the dark side, life is not going as the individual believes it should, they may find a state of depression arising. When the events or situations in the individual's life change from a high note to a low one, space is created for depression to arise. Any sudden unwelcome change in the individual's life who lives on the dark side may easily cause depression to creep in.

If the individual has their mind set on precisely what the individual wants to do, but circumstances will not allow it, the individual may easily drift into a lull of depression. Depression affects the individual's mental energy and narrows the vision of possibilities. Whenever there is an opportunity to fulfill a desire, and it does not manifest, a depressive state of mind may rise. In a busy life of accumulating material attractions and positions in this world, the individual living on the dark side tends to forget or ignore the needs of others. Fear of loss of any kind, vulnerability, or helplessness may cause an emotional depression to overshadow the individual; causing the individual to relentlessly attack those near and far. Preventive protection may become necessary – Impeachment.

# 11

# Soul

When darkness casts a vast shadow over a President's soul and those who would protect the individual, it is a dear price to pay. A soul, anyone's soul, is a dear price to pay. Why is it not worth the price of *anyone's* soul? In the simplest of terms, the soul is an individual expression manifesting as consciousness. The soul is the substance of (for the religious, God's) thoughts in action, expressing from the formless to the form, animating conscious human life.

The soul is the exhalation breath of its (God's) conscious source, and the breath (of God) is its eternal spiritual connection. The soul possesses the inherent ability to realize and to love itself. The soul is in the viable reflection from within awareness of each unique expression of consciousness.

The soul is the spark from within consciousness with awareness that ignites the rhythm of the vibratory energy. The life force and timekeeper determine the sojourn on the earth's plane of opposites. The soul preserves and holds the vibratory energy memory of all essential lessons in the individual expressions of consciousness.

The soul is the invisible fingerprint of an individual's spirituality, allowing it to be eternally known and identifiable. Impeachment cannot destroy the soul. Unfortunately, the individual living on the dark side comes close to doing it. Yes, it is a dear price to pay.

# 12

## A
## Remedy

Fortunately, there is a remedy for removing a President who lives on the dark side, impeachment and conviction. Additionally, there is a remedy for the individual living on the dark side to move to the light side. The following three chapters may allow the individual to move to the light side.

The following three chapters may also help the rest of us who must cope with impeachment and a divisive Nation. The restoration of a divided nation is the responsibility of each individual, and that restoration begins within each of us. So become acquainted with your Spiritual Center.

Humbly become aware of a quiet within your Spiritual Center. It is a powerful center of compassion, clarity, discernment, and wisdom. It is a powerhouse of gigantic proportions, one the mind cannot imagine nor the world can conceive. Its purity of vibrating energy can raise the most ordinary human being to the most magnificent one.

# 13

# **Your Spiritual Center**

*The Power Within You*

An old story goes something like this: After God had created humankind, God called one of the angels and asked the angel to hide the one thing God wished to conceal.

*"I have finished except for one thing: the mystery of life. Where shall you hide it?"* God asked the angel.

*"I will hide it in outer space,"* responded the excited angel.

*"No,"* God said, *"one day, it could easily be found there."*

*"All right, I will hide it on the moon. Surely it will not be found there?"*

*"No, no,"* said God, *"one day, someone will be able to look there also. Hmmm, I have it! Let's put it within them. They would never think to look there!"*

~~

There is a gentle, subtle vibrating center within you (in the center of the chest, between the breasts). It's called your Spiritual Center. Although often written about and discussed, your Spiritual Center's direct availability and easy access are *often* ignored. It is the most neglected entrance into the inner sanctuary of your being.

There are seven spiritual centers within the physical body. They begin at the base of the spine and end at the top of the head. These vibrating energy centers are located three below the Spiritual Center and three above it. Your Spiritual Center is the power-house influencing the centers above and below.

This pure vibrating energy center does not have a particular religious affiliation. Members from any religion, or none, may access it. Your Spiritual

Center connects all states and levels of consciousness. And depending on the state of consciousness you choose to realize — Christ, Buddha, Hindu, or any other — that is the one you may realize. It is amazing!

Though this powerful energy center is within you, it may seem strange and unfamiliar; you may shy away from this critical center for fear of the unknown. Fortunately, the Minute Meditation practice (chapter 14) gently guides you to the point where you may access your Spiritual Center. This is your birthright and may be reflected in your daily living.

Become aware of the power within your Spiritual Center. This essential power dissolves the darkness created by ignorance and the fear and hate that darkness breeds. You may realize a silence within that is available when you regularly connect with the power of your Spiritual Center.

Your Spiritual Center allows darkness to be dispelled, and the light of consciousness with awareness within you to be revealed. Leave your sorrow behind. Realize that you are not alone.

This world knows nothing of the power of your Spiritual Center. It cannot begin to comprehend all the strengths and actions in every vibration of your Spiritual Center. Enter through the door of your inner sanctuary. Do not deny yourself that which is yours by divine birthright. Look in the least expected place for the mystery of life: within *your* Spiritual Center. Here is where you may bask in the awareness of your spirituality.

You are invited to become aware of this powerhouse of possibilities that works through you, with you, and as you. In the powerhouse of your Spiritual Center, you are carried through the shadows of doubts, desires, and temptations of this world. No code is necessary to become aware of your Spiritual Center; no secret password, introduction, or referral is necessary. Your entrance is assured. It is up to you to become aware of it. It is always within *you*. Go for it!

# 14

# The Minute Meditation

Meditation may keep you in a calm, aware state of consciousness. When practicing the Minute Meditation, you may realize in the not dialoguing, conversing, or responding to the arising emotions, that you may be able to deal more effectively with arising emotions and maintain a calm, aware state. It is necessary to stay alert to prevent, not stop, but prevent the dialogue from occurring. Emotions arise with positive or negative memories. The strength of an emotion depends on the response to the memory. Most negative emotional responses require forgiveness to restore the energy to its natural neutral condition.

Forgiveness is unknowable to the mind. It is beyond the mind. The fruit of forgiveness is realized later when the memory of turmoil previously experienced arises again, and the vibratory energy is lightened. It is realized when the previous memory arises, and there is no longer a response. The memory is there, but responding to it is not.

The combination of no dialogue and forgiveness allows for immediate healing. It absolves absolutely the residue of suffering from the remaining memory by dissolving attachment. Hence, there is no emotional or psychological suffering. This is the benefit of forgiveness. The not dialoguing is the willingness to let go of the emotional attachment to a disturbing memory. The Minute Meditation will help you to become aware of forgiveness and move from the dark side.

Bringing conscious awareness to your Spiritual Center *area* is not a form of thought. A thought is thinking. As you become aware of your Spiritual Center *area,* you allow the thinking mind to rest.

The awareness is being moved back to your Spiritual Center *area* during a Minute Meditation practice. It is conscious awareness of becoming aware of your Spiritual Center *area.* Other meditation methods may use concentration with a "word/s" or concentration and awareness to reaffirm intention. The Minute Meditation uses awareness.

The Minute Meditation uses choice moved gently with a determined purpose. It does not require concentrated energy on a thought or word because *you* are the "Word," the word made flesh. The Minute Meditation allows for the bare awareness of your spirituality as it is. The practice guides you beyond the body and mind consciousness to the aware consciousness of your spirituality.

# 15

# The
# Practice

Practice the Minute Meditation at any time before a meal, at least two hours after a meal, and about an hour after liquid juices (the changing vibrating energy may interfere with digestion). Water is fine. Start your silent meditation practice with a few minutes allowing the practice time to extend naturally. Be consistent. Practice twice a day.

If, for any reason, you find it challenging to become aware of your Spiritual Center area, place your hand on your Spiritual Center *area* for the first few practices. Be patient. The practice is a silent, gentle one.

***The Practice:***

1. Sit comfortably. If you prefer, sit on a cushion on the floor. When sitting on a chair, you may wish to sit on a chair with arms for support. Close your eyes, and rest your hands gently on your lap. Slowly inhale deeply and

slowly exhale, relaxing the entire body. Continue to breathe normally.

**2.** Consciously become aware of your Spiritual Center area (center of the chest, between the breasts) and rest with awareness of your Spiritual Center *area*.

**3**. If thoughts or sensations arise, do not dialogue, converse, engage, or respond to their rising. Your attention is already there. Allow them to rise and again return to rest with awareness of your Spiritual Center *area*.

Do *not* label any of the rising thoughts, emotions, or senses. For example, when a bird sings, all that occurs is the rising sense of hearing. The identity "bird" is a conditioning label. Do not use it.

Continue the practice in this manner. No matter how often thoughts, emotions, or any of the senses rise, softly again become aware of your Spiritual Center *area*. The use of a meditation shawl is optional. It may be a useful tool to help turn you inward. At the end of silent meditation practice, take a few moments to become consciously aware of the mental and physical senses before returning to regular activity. Your spirituality is guiding you in and out of silent practice. Slowly, carefully, and lovingly your spirituality remembrance may be restored.

### The Second Practice

The second Minute Meditation practice of the day is your balanced maintenance connection. The importance of the Minute Meditation second daily practice cannot be overstated. Therefore, it is wise to take a little time out to go within twice a day.

You want to live from the inner to the outer without extreme ups and downs. Your morning Minute Meditation practice starts your day with stability. The second Minute Meditation practice maintains your stability.

As you go about your daily activities, you are bombarded with the many different frequencies (states) of consciousness. The world states of consciousness surround your every move. It is like walking through a minefield of infinite states of consciousness.

Your second Minute Meditation practice keeps you alert, steady and balanced throughout the latter part of the day. This is what allows you to identify and master the arising emotions. It is easy to drift or get caught up in other states of consciousness. Your Minute Meditation second practice period may protect you from drifting during your daily activities.

The one minute that you are willing to give to a second Minute Meditation practice will, in return, give you more pleasant hours during your day. You want to live a seamless life, do your second Minute Meditation practice, and stay aware. Live a seamless life.

# 16

# Exercises

The following are exercises you may wish to practice and ponder. They may increase your conscious awareness. So, use the ones you wish to practice.

## 1. Attention

Place your thumb and index finger together. Consciously focus your attention on the thumb touching the index finger, then shift your attention to the index finger touching the thumb.

## 2. Beyond Differences

For one day, do any household chore as though it were a sacred ritual.

## 3. Conscious Awareness - Oneness

Sit on a chair, and close your eyes. Stay aware of your bottom touching the chair seat, the chair feet touching the floor, the foundation of the house touching the earth, the earth connected to the neighborhood, the neighborhood within the city, the city within the state, the state within the nation, and the nation touching other countries.

## 4. Learn to Listen

Visit a friend. Allow the friend to converse without any interruptions. Allow the entire conversation to be about your friend.

## 5. Stamina - Awareness

Stand up straight with arms folded over your chest, relax, and be aware of your feet touching the ground. You may stand for hours by staying aware of your feet touching the ground.

## 6. The Personal Sense of I, me, my, mine.

For a half-day, do not use the words "I, me, my, or mine" in speech or writing.

If not, a half-day, an hour, or whatever is possible.

## 7. The Present

Start a day without any plans. Instead, do what is given to you to do each moment. Do not plan your next moment — there is none. Stay only in the present moment.

## 8. Mind — Resting

Talk less and listen more. Practice talking only when it is necessary. Stay aware of your thoughts rising less often when you speak less. Idle talk helps create a restless mind.

## 9. Not Distinguishable

The next time anyone praises you, consider it criticism; the next time anyone criticizes' you, consider it praise.

Eventually, praise or blame are the same.

## 10. When waking up

When waking up in the morning, note the first instant of awareness before you are conscious. Note the sequence: awareness, consciousness, mind, and its contents. In that first instant of awareness, there is no content.

## 11. Present, Past, and Future

Imagine you are on a street corner watching a parade approaching. You can see and are aware of its beginnings (present). Imagine you are at a second story watching the same parade. You can view and be aware of the passing (past) and more of the rest of the parade coming (future).

Imagine you have moved to the house's roof and can view the entire parade—present, past, and future. All are occurring simultaneously, and you are aware of it.

## 12. Value (Do this exercise only if you are permitted to use salt and pepper).

Label a salt shaker good and a pepper shaker bad. For lunch, use only what is labeled good. Then mark the salt shaker bad and the pepper shaker good. At dinnertime, use only what is labeled good. What changed the contents of the shakers' quality?

## 13. Timeless Day

When you have a free day, remove your wristwatch, and cover all clocks in the house. Live a day without time. If a day is too long, do it for a half day and experience freedom without time.

## 14. Sound

Gently cup your hand over your left ear. Listen carefully, and you may hear the universal "humming" sound. You may also do it with both ears cupped.

## 15. Write

Write on a piece of paper, "I am." Now, draw a diagonal line through the "I." Ponder what you have left.

## 16. Yes

Review a day or week of how often you said "No," and note if any "no" could have been a "yes." Would it have changed anything? How does it feel?

## 17. Silence

Sit comfortably, eyes closed, and place your attention on listening to hear a phone ring. Enjoy the silence.

# 17

# Major Points

1. The entire universe is consciousness.

2. All consciously created in the universe is relative to the world.

3. The conscious mind and body rise with Expansive Awareness.

4. You are not the mind, body, or anything in the universe.

5. The One becomes the many states of individual consciousness and the many return to the One.

6. You are not in the world; the universe is in your consciousness.

7. Consciousness changes and is limited. Awareness is changeless and limitless.

8. You may be aware of being conscious but you cannot be conscious of awareness.

9. This world, the earth plane of opposites, is not your permanent home.

10. All of this world must deteriorate and die. The life you are is immortal, eternal.

11. Stay aware; there is not anything that can attach to what or who you are. The mind's identifying attachment to anything causes suffering.

12. Always know you are not that which can taste, touch, smell, hear, feel, and think. What is true of you is true of all.

13. You may become aware of the Spiritual Center with the practice of the silent Minute Meditation.

14. You are an aware, free being, coming and going in experiences of dimensions in an aware consciousness. Wake up and live!

# **Conclusion**

Impeachment and conviction are the United States of America's Constitutional remedy for removing an unfit individual from the office of the Presidency. The United States Constitution is a magnificent work of art. Its words are written on a canvas of its people united — all people.

A Democratic Republic is a created fragile form of government. There are always the demons, inside and outside, who would attack its validity. However, it is an enduring form of governing when its people stand up and defend it.

The God who graced this Nation with a challenging Constitution also provided for its protection, the truth. There are many words of praise and asking for God to Bless America. God *has* Blessed America. Is there a brave individual who will step forward and say, "Thank you?"

# Author / Translator

**Carla R. Mancari** is an author, translator, life guide, and teacher. She seeks to improve the self-confidence and self-esteem of individuals from all walks of life so that they can meet life's challenges. For more than 45 years, she has guided individuals in understanding life's spiritual principles, activities, and rising emotions in their private and daily lives. Carla is the recipient of the Christ Consciousness Meditation and the Minute Meditation. Although she had never attended high school and was labeled a retarded child, she attained two University degrees: a B.A. from the University of South Carolina in Columbia, South Carolina, and an MEd from South Carolina State University in Orangeburg, South Carolina. Carla studied at Brigham Young University and attended the School of the Americas in Switzerland.

Carla led a class action lawsuit in the United States Supreme Court to protect minorities' rights (Morton v. Mancari, 1973) and was a certified psychologist. She served in the United States Air Force. Traveling worldwide for many years, Carla studied with Christian, Hindu, and Buddhist masters. She was a guest on the Larry King Radio Show and a guest lecturer at various colleges, professional groups, book clubs, and at book signings. Carla gained national recognition when featured in *Good Housekeeping*, "The Education of Carla Mancari, 1969." It chronicled her life in 1967-68 when she was the first white woman to receive a Master's degree from the all-Black South Carolina State College in Orangeburg, South Carolina. She is the author of many books. Carla's greatest joy is helping individuals realize their self-worth, unique gifts/talents, and full potential, and wake up to their spiritual reality.

# Books

**Mancari, Carla R.**, *The Lessons: How to Understand Spiritual Principles, Spiritual Activities and Rising Emotions, A Comprehensive Collection.* Celestial Literary Group, 2026.

- - - *Christ Consciousness Meditation Practice: Pocket Size.* Celestial Literary Group, 2026.

- - - *Loneliness.* Celestial Literary Group, 2026.

- - - *Racism, Antisemitism+: A Disease of the Mind.* Celestial Literary Group, 2026.

- - - *The Christ Consciousness Meditation Teaching Guide.* Celestial Literary Group, 2026.

- - - *Metaphysical Questions with Answers from the Christ Consciousness.* Celestial Literary Group, 2026.

- - - *When Jesus Is the Guru: A Wayward Christian's Spiritual Walk*. Celestial Literary Group, 2010.

- - - *Eco-You: A Power of One, Improve Your Health, Improve Your Life*. Celestial Literary Group, 2019.

- - - *Walking on the Grass: A White Woman In A Black World*. Celestial Literary Group, 2016.

- - - *Abortion and The Bible: The Abortion Dilemma: A Scriptural Response, A Woman's Spirituality*. Celestial Literary Group, 2017.

- - - *Racism: The Pain of Invisibility*. Celestial Literary Group, 2017.

- - - *The Rising Emotions: Understanding and Mastering Them*. Celestial Literary Group, 2017.

- - - *The Mystical Path: The Serious Student*. Celestial Literary Group, 2017.

- - - *Spiritual Principles: Understanding, Realizing, and Living Them*. Celestial Literary Group, 2018.

- - - *Climate Change: Consciousness Change*. Celestial Literary Group, 2017.

- - - *Words: Locks On The Door or Keys To The Kingdom*. Celestial Literary Group, 2018.

- - - *Aging: Physical to the Mystical*. Celestial Literary Group, 2018.

- - - *Divine Love: Your Nature*. Celestial Literary Group, 2018.

- - - *The Lazarus Rising: The Kundalini – A Rising Dormant Energy*. Celestial Literary Group, 2018.

- - - *Depression: Hopelessness – A Disconnection*. Celestial Literary Group, 2018.

- - - *Jesus Christ: Teacher*. Celestial Literary Group, 2018.

- - - *The Mystical Surrender: Giving In*. Celestial Literary Group, 2018.

- - - *Death Ain't Dead: Empty Graves*. Celestial Literary Group, 2018.

- - - *Common Decency: Your DNA*. Celestial Literary Group, 2018.

- - - *Christians?: Common Decency.* Celestial Literary Group, 2018.

- - - *Beyond Buddhism: Meditations.* Celestial Literary Group, 2018.

- - - *Exit: Get Ready, Set, Go.* Celestial Literary Group, 2018.

- - - *Meditation: Good For You.* Celestial Literary Group, 2018.

- - - *How To Love "You": Begins with You.* Celestial Literary Group, 2018.

- - - *Consciousness: Yours.* Celestial Literary Group, 2018.

- - - *Suicide: Understanding It.* Celestial Literary Group, 2018.

- - - *Detachment: Realizations.* Celestial Literary Group, 2018.

- - - *Detachment: Christian.* Celestial Literary Group, 2018.

- - - *Sexual Abuse By The Church – Its Root, Coerced Celibacy.* Celestial Literary Group, 2018.

- - - *Guns and Guts: The Courage To Act.* Celestial Literary Group, 2018.

- - - *Jesus, The Way: A Mystical Understanding.* Celestial Literary Group, 2019.

- - - *Motivation: Self-Motivated.* Celestial Literary Group, 2019.

- - - *Totally Free: Is Killing Me.* Celestial Literary, Group, 2018.

- - - *A 30-Second Meditation For Teenagers.* Celestial Literary Group, 2018.

- - - *A 30-Second Meditation For Seniors.* Celestial Literary Group, 2017.

- - - *The Five Faces Of Love. Celestial Literary Group, 2019.*

- - - *Angel In The House.* Celestial Literary Group, 2019 (A Children's Book).

- - - *Put It In The Bible: Prayerful Requests.* Celestial Literary Group, 2019.

- - - *Hate: A Dark Emotion.* Celestial Literary Group, 2019.

- - - *Greed: It's Addictive.* Celestial Literary Group, 2019.

- - - *On Being Young: Choices.* Celestial Literary Group, 2019.

- - - *Gratitude: Expressed, Sincere.* Celestial Literary Group, 2019.

- - - *Humor: A Necessity.* Celestial Literary Group, 2019.

- - - *A Christian: Are You One?* Celestial Literary Group, 2019.

- - - *Habit: How To Switch Meditation Practices.* Celestial Literary Group, 2019.

- - - *Impeachment: Living On The Dark Side.* Celestial Literary Group, 2019.

- - - *The Jesus I Know.* Celestial Literary Group, 2019.

- - - *Grace: Spirit And Truth.* Celestial Literary Group, 2019.

- - - *Temptation.* Celestial Literary Group, 2019.

- - - *The Christian Journey: Teacher Student Relationship.* Celestial Literary Group, 2019.

- - - *The Beloved: Who Is The Beloved?* Celestial Literary Group, 2019.

- - - *What Now, Lord? Enlightenment.* Celestial Literary Group, 2019.

- - - *What If I Were Gay?* Celestial Literary Group, 2019.

- - - *Mother Mary: Mother of Jesus.* Celestial Literary Group, 2019.

- - - *I Remember America.* Celestial Literary Group, 2019.

- - - *The Overcoming: Jesus.* Celestial Literary Group, 2019.

- - - *When Faith Is Not Enough.* Celestial Literary Group, 2019.

- - - *The Plane of Opposites: The Work.* Celestial Literary Group, 2020.

- - - *Crisis.* Celestial Literary Group, 2020.

- - - *Grief: Gut-Wrenching Emotion.* Celestial Literary Group, 2020.

- - - *God.* Celestial Literary Group, 2020.

- - - *Regrets: Do You Have Any?* Celestial Literary Group, 2020.

- - - *1968, 1968,1968: The Mind of A Racist.* Celestial Literary Group, 2020.

- - - *Satan.* Celestial Literary Group, 2020.

- - - *Practice Practice: Meditation.* Celestial Literary Group, 2021.

- - - *Christians Without Jesus: Prodigal Son's Journey.* Celestial Literary Group, 2021.

- - - *From Here To There.* Celestial Literary Group, 2021.

- - - *An Awakening Path: Christian Spiritual Principles.* Celestial Literary Group, 2021.

- - - *Holy Scriptures: Uplifting, Inspiring and Comforting.* Celestial Literary Group, 2021.

- - - *Male Female: The Split Soul.* Celestial Literary Group, 2021.

- - - *The Inner Message: Theological Mystical State.* Celestial Literary Group, 2021.

- - - *A Guide To Understanding Mind's Contents And Realizations.* Celestial Literary Group, 2021.

- - - *A Sister's Laughter: Oh! How I Miss It* Celestial Literary Group, 2021.

- - - *Churches: Are They Necessary?* Celestial Literary Group, 2021.

- - - *Metaphysical: Stories and Poems.* Celestial Literary Group, 2021.

- - - *Jesus, Jesus, Jesus.* Celestial Literary Group, 2021.

- - - *The Disciple and The Mystical Guide.* Celestial Literary Group, 2021.

- - - *The Holy Trinity: 1+1+1=1, No Mystery.* Celestial Literary Group, 2021.

- - - *Fear of Jesus: Why?.* Celestial Literary Group, 2021.

- - - *Symbols and Rituals: Christian.* Celestial Literary Group, 2021.

- - - *Christian Minute Meditation.* Celestial Literary Group, 2021.

- - - *Sin!.* Celestial Literary Group, 2021.

- - - *Compassion.* Celestial Literary Group, 2021.

- - - *Silence.* Celestial Literary Group, 2021.

- - - *The Spiritual Zone.* Celestial Literary Group, 2022.

- - - *The Bible Scriptures: Mystical Understanding.* Celestial Literary Group, 2022.

- - - *Lead Us Not Into Temptation: The Lord's Prayer.* Celestial Literary Group, 2022.

- - - *Let's Talk About Jesus, Or Not.* Celestial Literary Group, 2022.

- - - *For The Love of Jesus: Come Back To Your Church.* Celestial Literary Group, 2022.

- - - *Abortion, When Life Does Not Begin! Exodus 21:22-25.* Celestial Literary Group, 2022.

- - - *Morton vs. Mancari: A Plaintiff's Response: How An Average Joe (woman) Landed In The US Supreme Court.* Celestial Literary Group, 2022.

- - - *Christian Spiritual Exercises: The Inner Journey.* Celestial Literary Group, 2023.

- - - *The Kingdom Of God – A Gift.* Celestial Literary Group, 2023.

- - - *An Expression of Love.* Celestial Literary Group, 2023.

- - - *Choices and Decisions On a Spiritual Journey.* Celestial Literary Group, 2024.

- - - *Love Your Enemies: How Can You Do That?.* Celestial Literary Group, 2024.

- - - *Outer Space and Inner Space Travel.* Celestial Literary Group, 2024.

- - - *God – Love: Poets Write About It.* Celestial Literary Group, 2024.

- - - *The Still Small Voice, You Can Hear It.* Celestial Literary Group, 2024.

- - - *The Resurrection: Rising Beyond Body Consciousness.* Celestial Literary Group, 2024.

- - - *Sexual Spiritual Intercourse: Oneness.* Celestial Literary Group, 2024.

- - - *Child Of God: In Spirit and Truth.* Celestial Literary Group, 2024.

- - - *"My Child," Blessed Mother Mary's.* Celestial Literary Group, 2024.

- - - *Strait Gate and Narrow Way: "Few There Be That Find It".* Celestial Literary Group, 2024.

- - - *Strait Gate and Narrow Way: "Few There Be That Find It", Pocket*

*Size.* Celestial Literary Group, 2024.

- - - *The End Of The Beginning, Our Spiritual Journey.* Celestial Literary Group, 2024.

- - - *A Cat Story.* Celestial Literary Group, 2025.

**Mancari, Carla. R.** *and* **Carpenter, Mary B.** *Scriptural Reference For - The Lessons, A Comprehensive Collection.* Celestial Literary Group, 2026.

- - -*The Minute Meditation, Book 1: It Is Profound!* Celestial Literary Group, 2022.

- - -*The Minute Meditation, Book 2: Workbook, It Is Profound!.* The Celestial Literary Group, 2022.

- - - *The Minute Meditation, It Is Profound! Book 3: The Essentials.* Celestial Literary Group, 2022.

- - - *The Minute Meditation, It Is Profound! Book 4: A Diet For The Soul.* Celestial Literary Group, 2022.

- - - *The Minute Meditation, It Is Profound! Book 5: The Three of You, You Are Never Alone.* Celestial Literary Group, 2022.

- - - *The Minute Meditation, It Is Profound! Book 6: Pocket Size.* Celestial Literary Group, 2022.

- - - *The Minute Meditation, It Is Profound! Book 7 – Teaching Guide.* Celestial Literary Group, 2022.

- - - *The Minute Meditation, It Is Profound! Book 8 – The 4th Chakra.* Celestial Literary Group, 2026.

- - - *Spirituality: Yours.* Celestial Literary Group, 2021.

- - - *Dreams: States of Consciousness.* Celestial Literary Group, 2021.

- - - *A Christian Service With A Silent Christian Meditation.* Celestial Literary Group, 2024.

**Casey-Martus, Sandra, and Mancari, Carla R.** *The Lessons, How to Understand Spiritual Principles, Spiritual Activities and Rising Emotions, Lessons with Stories Along a Spiritual Journey.* Celestial Literary Group, 2026.

# NOTES